Kathy Prendergast The End and The Beginning

with an essay by Francis McKee

MERRELL PUBLISHERS
IN ASSOCIATION WITH THE IRISH MUSEUM OF MODERN ART

Published on the occasion of the exhibition
**Kathy Prendergast: The End and The
Beginning** at Irish Museum of Modern Art,
Dublin, 1 December 1999 – 26 March 2000.

First published in 1999 by
Merrell Publishers Ltd
42 Southwark Street, London SE1 1UN
in association with
Irish Museum of Modern Art
Royal Hospital, Military Road
Kilmainham, Dublin 8

Distributed in the USA and Canada by
Rizzoli International Publishers, Inc.
through St Martin's Press, 175 Fifth Avenue,
New York, New York 10010

British Library Cataloguing-in-
Publication Data

McKee, Francis
Kathy Prendergast : the end and the
beginning
1.Prendergast, Kathy, 1958– – Criticism and
interpretation 2.Art, Modern – 20th century –
Ireland
I.Title
709.2

ISBN 1 85894 096 6

Edited by Brenda McParland
and Julian Honer
Photography by Edward Woodman
and Dennis Mortell
Designed by Peter B. Willberg
at Clarendon Road Studio

Produced by Merrell Publishers
Printed and bound in Italy

The Irish Museum of Modern Art is grateful
to those who have generously lent their
works for the exhibition from private and
public collections. In particular, we should
like to thank John Hannan, Anne and
William J. Hokin, Kerlin Gallery, Dubln, The
Arts Council of Ireland and Robert Miller
Gallery, New York. Our thanks also to Kathy
Prendergast, Francis McKee, Susan Corr
and Edward Woodman for their involvement
and assistance.

The artist would like to thank Dan Knight,
Angela Prendergast, Terry Prendergast,
Cecily Brennan, Karen O'Conor, John
Wilson, Elisabeth Magill, Yuko Shiraishi,
Anna O'Sullivan, Peter Hendrick, Ken and
Davy at the Kerlin Gallery, Alex Elder of
Batholomew, Paul Coldwell, George Whale,
Barbara Rauch and Naren Barfield at the
Intergration of Computers within Fine Art
Practice at Camberwell College of Arts and
Chelsea College of Art and Design, Emma,
Harriet and Debbie of Wallace Sewell, Dr
Catherine Nash, Inder and Rachel of John
Oliver, Bruce Cameron, Frances Morris,
Edward Woodman, Francis McKee and last
but not least Brenda McParland, Catherine
Marshall and all the staff at the Irish
Museum of Modern Art.

Front cover:
The End and The Beginning II, 1997
(see page 99)

Back cover:
After (detail), 1999
(see page 111)

Frontispiece:
Still Life (detail), 1999
(see page 95)

Kathy Prendergast The End and The Beginning

Th·

Contents

Lost
1999
compass reworked by artist
6 × 4.5 × 1 cm

Foreword

Kathy Prendergast was born in Dublin in 1958. She studied Fine Art at the National College of Art and Design in Dublin from 1976 to 1980 and from 1982 to 1983 and Sculpture at the Royal College of Art in London from 1983 to 1986. Prendergast has lived and worked in London since 1982 and is considered to be one of the leading artists of her generation to have emerged from Ireland. She has exhibited in solo and group exhibitions since 1982, including at the Douglas Hyde Gallery, Dublin, the Angles Gallery, Los Angeles, and the Camden Arts Centre and the Tate Gallery, London. In 1995 Prendergast was one of two artists to represent Ireland at the Venice Biennale, where she won the prestigious Premio 2000 prize.

This book marks Kathy Prendergast's first solo museum exhibition and focuses on work from 1992 to 1999, a period in which interesting developments took place in her work.

The impetus for this exhibition and book came largely from the purchase of the 'City Drawings' in 1995 by the Irish Museum of Modern Art, Dublin. The 'City Drawings' are a series of drawings of contemporary maps of all the world's capital cities. This ambitious project began in 1992 and is currently a work in progress that will constitute 180 drawings when complete. This exhibition will display 113 completed drawings, the largest number to be exhibited yet, and marks the first showing of the drawings in Ireland.

The End and The Beginning explores the 'City Drawings' and other works made during the same period, such as small- and large-scale sculpture, photoworks, series of pencil drawings of lakes and rivers of Ireland, and computer-generated atlas and map works.

The themes in Prendergast's work are as expansive and poignant as the cycle of human life and engage in issues from fertility, evident in Still Life (1999); childhood, ageing and the passing of time, as seen in such pieces as Untitled (1984; depicting a baby's jumper), The Endless Goodbye (1998) and The End and The Beginning I and II (1997); to works associated with spirituality, death, mourning and loss, such as *Prayer Gloves*, *Grave Blanket* (both 1997) and *Negative Space* (1999). Recent works such as *Love Table* (1999), *Love Object* (1999), *After* (1999) and *Secret Kiss* (1999) evoke nostalgic memories of cherished love. In earlier works the female figure was present in such works as *Seabed* (1980), *Waiting* (1980) and *Body Maps* (1983), whereas in works since 1992 this is replaced by a human presence.

Prendergast works with a huge variety of materials, and the scale of her works range from life-size installations to tiny sculptures. In the past she has used materials as varied as string, wool, paint, eggs, photography, fabric, found objects and hair, and she is currently experimenting with blown glass, computer-generated images and video. Her drawings and works on paper demonstrate great dexterity, and the majority of her sculptures retain a hand-made, craft-like quality emphasizing the uniqueness of each object and revealing the labour-intensive nature of the work, regardless of its size.

I should like to thank a number of individuals and institutions for their assistance and co-operation in realizing this project. First, our sincere gratitude to the artist, Kathy Prendergast, who has given so generously of her time to the organization of this exhibition and who has been a pleasure to work with. Over the past year she has shared her range of works and her exceptional vision and has participated in every stage of the planning process. Our thanks to the owners of Kathy Prendergast's work who have agreed to lend to the exhibition and also to Anna O'Sullivan, the Robert Miller Gallery, the Kerlin Gallery, the Arts Council of Ireland, the Arts Council of England, the Tate Gallery, Susan Corr and Edward Woodman. My thanks also to Francis McKee for his enlightening text, which provides a new perspective on Kathy Prendergast at an appropriate time in her career.

Brenda McParland
Head of Exhibitions
Irish Museum of Modern Art

To Hide in Plain Sight Francis McKee

1

In a recent article entitled 'The Agency of Mapping', James Corner argues that mapping at its best is a creative practice that "unfolds potential; it re-makes territory over and over again, each time with new and diverse consequences". Many maps are simply tracings of what already exists, he says, but the best maps reveal potential futures for the landscape they describe. He then goes on to quote the philosophers Gilles Deleuze and Félix Guattari, who proclaimed: "Make a map not a tracing!"

This approach to map-making is similar to that in Prendergast's maps of capital cities of the world that form her 'City Drawings' series and, in different ways, to 'The Lakes of Ireland', 'The Rivers of Ireland', *Lost* and *Empty Atlas*. At first, the 'City Drawings' seem to resemble the "tracings" to which James Corner refers. They do trace the streets of each of the capital cities of the world and they do derive from existing street maps of those cities.

The resemblance ends there, however, as Prendergast has manipulated the scale of several of the maps to retain a continuity in the overall sequence of drawings, and this alone begins to remove them from the accurate, faithful world of the 'trace'. Most importantly, when we look at these maps we are aware of the amount of information Prendergast has removed from the image. The lines indicating streets intersect each other and intertwine like arteries, but she has eradicated all signs of buildings, parks, and facilities that add meaning to such a map. Moreover, the drawings float in the middle of a white sheet, the lines ending abruptly in space, denying the viewer any sense of how the city might connect to its surrounding hinterland.

By paring the city maps down to their bare bones, Prendergast reveals potential lines of communication in each city that might otherwise have been obscured by the indication of buildings, districts and street names – all of which are burdened by preconceptions.

James Corner's article concludes as follows:

'City Drawings'
(Amsterdam, Netherlands; detail)
1992 (ongoing series)

… mapping is not the indiscriminate, blinkered accumulation and endless array of data, but rather an extremely shrewd and tactical enterprise, a practice of relational reasoning that intelligently unfolds new realities out of existing constraints, quantities, facts and conditions. The artistry lies in the use of technique, in the way in which things are framed and set up. Through reformulating things differently, novel and inventive possibilities emerge … The agency of mapping lies in its cunning exposure and engendering of new sets of possibilities.

By paring down the maps in 'City Drawings', Prendergast reveals an underlying pattern in each of the world's capitals. Often the founding history of the city is laid bare: the convoluted centre of a mediaeval town or the grid formation of a new world system.

The key element that all the 'City Drawings' have in common, however, is the simple fact that each reveals a network of roads promising access and communication for the citizens of the city. As such, the drawings represent more than a physical landscape. Their emphasis on a network focuses our attention on the aspirations of the cities' populations and those of the cities' rulers. Because each drawing represents a capital city, these aspirations acquire national significance as communication within each city deltas out to the surrounding countryside and the larger network of towns, villages and ports that comprise each country.

The aspiration towards effective communication and travel evident in these drawings is a utopian one. Behind it lies the hope that such communication will lead to prosperity and a cohesive, unified social order. In our more recent move into the information age, such aspirations have been transposed to the newly emerging information networks and the world-wide web. Mapping remains just as important in this modern landscape, and the arterial networks of cities have provided a model for electricity grids, fibre-optic systems, computer circuitry and the creation of virtual spaces. In this context, Prendergast's 'City Drawings' can be seen as emblems of the free-flowing networks that could transform our society if they remain open and accessible.

Armand Mattelart, a professor of Information and Communication Sciences, sums up the dangers to our information networks as follows:

> In 1948 Norbert Wiener, the founder of cybernetics, diagnosed the structuring power of the 'information' network; he was convinced that future society would be organised around it. If humanity wished to avoid a return to the barbarism of the war it had to appropriate that power. While the mathematician's ideal was incarnated in the 'information society', he warned the public against the dangers of abusing it. Its principal enemy was entropy, or the tendency in nature to destroy the orderly and to hasten biological deterioration and social disorder ... information, the machines which process it and the network they create were the only things which could resist blockage to circulation, which is exactly what entropy produces. An information society must be a society where information circulates freely. It is by definition incompatible with restriction and secrecy, with inequality of access and the transformation of circulation into commodity. To encourage these is to promote entropy, to hinder human progress.

Each of Prendergast's 'City Drawings' reinforces an image of free circulation, and the very repetition in the work's long sequence underlines the global significance of such interlocking networks. Her drawings imply both the utopian potential of every capital city and the entropy that endangers that vision.

The civic and public nature of such an enterprise could possibly seem abstract and of little personal relevance to the individual viewer of these images. However, there is a more private route to an understanding of these works, and it lies in their resemblance to the nerve maps of the human brain. Approaching the works across a gallery, before any awareness of their titles, the drawings bear a striking similarity to the now-familiar web-like images of the nervous system. One psychiatrist describes the minutiae of the brain like this:

> The main work center of the neuron is the cell body, which contains the nucleus of the cell ... The cell bodies send out tiny fingers of branching fibers called 'dendrites' (treelike structures). This treelike web around the cell body enormously increases its ability to receive information, since other cells can communicate either to the cell body itself or to its dendrites.
>
> In addition to the dendrites, the cell body sends out long, tubular projections – the axons – that it uses to communicate with other neurons .... The axons are the 'wires' of the nervous system ... [p.125]

In the early part of the twentieth century, one of the founders of neuroscience, Santiago Ramón y Cajal, explored various staining methods that would allow him to isolate these webs of nerves and map them. He recalls the experience, saying:

> I was fully convinced that, in order to make a significant advance in the knowledge of the structure of the nerve centres, it was absolutely necessary to make use of procedures capable of showing the most delicate rootlets of the nerve fibres vigorously and selectively coloured upon a clear background. It is well known that the gray matter is formed by something like a very dense felt of excessively fine threads ...

Cajal's eventual success in identifying these interlocking tree-like structures provided the foundation of contemporary conceptions of the brain and its network messaging system. A keen amateur artist, he drew and painted the exposed nerves himself, laying them out on the white page in a manner similar to Kathy Prendergast's pared-down drawings.

Through Cajal's pioneering work, new formulations of theories of human memory have quickly evolved. As the psychiatrist Nancy Andreasen puts it:

> Most research suggests that short-term memory involves setting up brief reverberating circuits through the electrical transmission of nerves, while long-term memory probably involves a more permanent process represented by actual physical changes in the brain, through the creation of new connections between nerve cells ...

Cajal's nerve maps then represent the routes taken by memories through the brain, and in the cases of connecting lines may represent the 'growth' of a long-term memory. In the light of such research, Prendergast's drawings begin to take on some elements of portraiture – potential images of personal memory maps.

This relationship to memory remains strong even if we consider her drawings solely as maps of cities. By choosing capital cities of the world, Prendergast subtly points to centuries of colonization and imperial influence. The memory of such invasion can be seen in the repeated patterns in the drawings, where new world cities imitate the outline and form of the cities of their distant rulers. This is perhaps clearest in the grid cities, where the pragmatic cross-sections retain the memory of the military camps of the invaders and the exported enlightenment values of Europe. Even the navigation of a city's street, then, engages the citizen in a memory-trace stretching back through hundreds of years. Ironically, too, as citizens memorize the street plan they internalize it and feed it through the nerve maps of their brains.

2

One of the unseen difficulties in creating a work such as 'City Drawings' lies in the sourcing of maps for each capital city in the world. In our daily use of city maps we approach them as items that will help us navigate large networks of city streets, one-way systems and major junctions. In the recent past, however, a city map was perceived as a dangerous source of information for enemies. In Moscow, for instance, it was considered an act of espionage for a foreigner to make a map of the city – thereby rendering it more susceptible to invasion. In 1934 the American major-league baseball all-stars toured Japan. On 29 November they played at the Omiya Grounds north of the city. The American catcher Moe Berg cried off sick from the game, and while Tokyo was preoccupied with Babe Ruth's performance, he made his way to the roof of St Luke's International Hospital, one of the tallest buildings in the city. There, he photographed the entire cityscape, focusing in particular on industrial installations and on the Japanese warships anchored in the bay. On his return to America, he borrowed snaps taken by several of his teammates and, along with with his own photographs, these were studied by an anxious intelligence service in Washington.

Later, during the Second World War, there were countless stories of road signs being turned to misdirect invading forces. These anecdotes not only demonstrate the secrecy that can surround city mapping, but they also hint at the ways in which vulnerable sites in full view can be hidden most effectively if their orientation is deliberately confused.

With the advent of satellites and their ever-increasing power to depict detail, however, mapping a city became a simple task. At this point camouflage became much more important, drawing on the lessons learnt both from the animal world and from twentieth-century military history. The Darwinian drive that induces animals to evolve camouflage schemes was first codified in 1909 by an American artist, Abbott Thayer, in his book *Concealing Coloration in the Animal Kingdom*. H.G. Wells summarized Thayer's work, saying:

> *He was the first to realise the value of what may be called ruptive coloration — bold pattern which breaks up the form and outline of an animal into irregular and meaningless pieces … The same principle, in exaggerated degree, was adopted for concealing guns, ships, and so on in the War. As an anti-submarine measure, an interesting variation was adopted. Ships were painted in bold patterns, usually in black, white, and blue, so as to give, through false perspective effects, a wrong idea of their course; and this made it much harder for the submarine to take up the correct position for attack.*

Hiding secrets in full view became an art. In *Negative Space* Kathy Prendergast assumes all the skills of this art and employs them to explore the unconscious and unspoken truths that lie concealed in all our lives. The box in the installation has the dimensions of a grave and is decorated with a funereal, black-and-cream wallpaper. Rather than sinking into the ground, however, this grave-like form erupts into the space, disguised by the wallpaper, which allows it to blend in with the similarly decorated walls of the room. The grave becomes an invisible monument, a mournful piece of architecture that mimics its neighbour (*Still Life*), just as the temple-like tombs of the Père Lachaise cemetery in Paris echo the architecture of that city. Describing the psychological need for such forms, cultural theorist Peggy Phelan writes that

*The monument and the pyramid are where they are to cover up a place, to fill in a void: the one left by death. Death must not appear: it must not take place: let tombs cover it up and take its place …
One plays dead so that death will not come. So nothing will happen and time will not take place.*

Prendergast's camouflaged tomb provokes a complex response. It implies that death is hidden but constantly with us, camouflaged to stalk us more effectively. It also implies that we have disguised death and the dead ourselves, burying painful memories. The tomb's eruption into the room suggests the surge of repressed mourning that lies in our unconscious. The dream-like presence of the sculpture allows us to acknowledge the fact of death, while the optical illusion of its camouflage lets us render it invisible again. This, as Phelan points out, is part of the tomb's ambivalent function: "In order to forestall or forget death, architecture invents the tomb which both distracts us from the specificity of the dead body and underlines the stone cold fact of death itself." The almost regal, stately design of the wallpaper Prendergast has chosen for her sculpture underlines this ambivalence. The ornate black-and-cream fleur-de-lis pattern is sombre enough for an undertaker's parlour. At the same time, there is a complexity and profusion of detail in the design, a riot of flowers and feathery petals that seem to celebrate life and nature.

This duality allows Prendergast's work to tap into very deeply rooted approaches to death, much in the same way that Joyce's *Finnegans Wake* used a dream narrative to celebrate the death and resurrection of a Dublin publican. The wake traditions themselves reflect a desire both to mourn and to party. Throughout history, in Ireland in particular, there has been a series of semi-comical rituals associated with the mourning of the recently deceased. Seán O'Súilleabháin, an Irish folklorist, describes countless examples of games played specifically at wakes, such as 'Building the Bridge':

> *Twelve men or so stood out on the floor and formed into two lines of six each, facing one another. Each man took hold of the two hands of the man opposite, thus forming the bridge from which the game took its name. The bridge had now to be tested for strength. Another player mounted on the crossed hands and walked to and fro along them. Finding no apparent fault with its construction, he dismounted. Somebody would then suggest that the bridge be tested to see if it would take a flood of water through its eye. This would be done by some rogue who sluiced the legs and feet of the players with a bucketful of dirty water.*

O'Súilleabháin concludes that the games, drinking and dancing common at the wake were stimulated by a fear of the dead and a desire to placate the spirit of the deceased, offering a final proof of their esteem in their physical presence.

The playfulness of the wake and its ambivalence towards death permeate many of Prendergast's works, such as *Love Object*, *Love Table* and *Secret Kiss*. Each has a dark, dream-like aspect offering mournful games tinged with grief. On a larger scale, the relationship between her *Negative Space* and *Still Life* becomes a witty, labyrinthine dialogue as each work plays off the other. In these last two works, both boxes are built to a similar grave-size scale, but as the *Negative Space* operates by stealth, *Still Life* works through revelation. There is no camouflage on the white exterior and the viewer is invited to open the small shutters at eye level and peer inside through a confessional-like grille. Within the box, eggshells are suspended from the ceiling, creating a faint clacking noise when they move. The work raises an immediate cluster of associations: the Catholic reference to the confessional box, the symbolism of eggs, surrealist art. There is even a reminder of Marcel Duchamp's final work, *Étant Donées*, an assemblage visible only through a peep-hole.

Still Life (detail)
1999

Beyond the initial impact of these references, *Still Life* opens a broader dialogue with *Negative Space*. There at first seems to be an opposition between the two works – one full of eggs representing life, one funereal. On closer inspection, however, they begin to reveal a more complex relationship.

Both pieces resemble tombs and the monumental character of *Still Life* is perhaps even stronger because of its stark white shroud. While the black-and-cream wallpaper design of the *Negative Space* discloses a profusion of flora and burgeoning nature, the whiteness of *Still Life* becomes deathly, suggesting oblivion through its emptiness and lack of colour. Likewise, the eggshells within evoke an initial sense of life but gradually we become aware that they are emptied and encased in a memorial. In this context, the title of the piece, too – *Still Life* – assumes darker connotations. There are echoes of the Dutch seventeenth-century tradition of the still-life painting in which eggs, lemons, oysters and other foodstuffs functioned as symbols of death, lust and human transience. The egg is often thought of as a symbol of rebirth because of its prominence in Easter rituals, and with the commercial emphasis today on chocolate eggs the darker side of this association is often forgotten. In a wider history of food, however, these references are still recorded:

Decorated eggs are not by any means all meant to be kept, most are eaten. However, in Romania and the Ukraine the shells are saved to be thrown into the river (an ancient gesture with various different kinds of significance). The shells go down into the other world to tell the dead to be of good cheer: Christ is risen, and all at home are rejoicing. The gypsies 'write' eggs for the dead, ornamenting them with sinuous or broken lines which only the departed can decipher. The eggs are taken to graves, and the departed can thus still share in family joys. In Greece, on the afternoon of Easter Day, people go to the graveyard to eat eggs, taking a plate with the share of the dead on it.

The eggs in Prendergast's *Still Life* have such links to death. They work as a *memento mori* and as a reminder of rebirth, just as the title *Still Life* can evoke the idea of a still birth or assert that there is still life despite adversity.

3

Both *Negative Space* and *Still Life* evoke a series of ideas and associations beyond rational interpretation. This is a characteristic shared by many of Prendergast's other works, each seeming to spring from a personal, coded impulse, but each resonating at a common pitch for the public viewer. Her maps and objects chart the territory of the unconscious, making apparent a fluid, volatile world that ebbs and flows beneath the surface of everyday life.

Picking up the funereal echoes of the two large installations, smaller pieces such as *Prayer Gloves*, *Grave Blanket*, *The Endless Goodbye* and *After* extend the meditation of mortality. They touch quietly on the anxieties of death that shadow daily routines. Domestic items of comfort and warmth – gloves, pillows, blankets – become entwined in a sombre evocation of loss.

Prendergast subtly shifts each object from its natural place in the world, making it strange to us again. In doing this, she demonstrates an affinity for the Surrealists' use of the object in their art. Appropriating found objects and transforming domestic materials to construct unexpected totems, the Surrealists playfully created entirely new categories for 'things'. In the 1936 exhibition of Surrealist objects in Paris, these objects were described as "natural, interpreted, perturbed, found, found interpreted, American, oceanic, mathematical, readymade and readymade aided,

Prayer Gloves
1998

and Surrealist". André Breton, one of the most prominent of the Surrealists, argued that these dream-like objects were made to oppose the certainties of the conscious world and its utilitarian commodities. The Surrealist object, he said, was designed to "demolish these concrete trophies which are so odious, to throw further discredit on those creatures and things of reason". By choosing recognizable, everyday objects and transforming them, the Surrealists challenged the mundaneness of the domestic world. In a description of the effects of montage technique, Breton goes on to say that

> *It is the marvelous faculty of attaining two widely separate realities without departing from the realm of our experience, of bringing them together, and drawing a spark from their contact … and of disorienting us in our memory by depriving us of a frame of reference …*

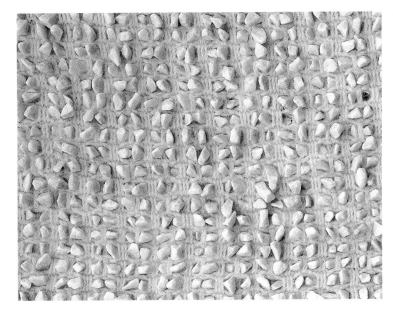

Grave Blanket (Version I) (detail)
1997

Such a description could also be applied to the effect generated by the objects of Kathy Prendergast. Her choice of object often reflects the domestic – a table, a chair, a hairbrush, gloves *etc.* – yet the transformation of these objects brings the everyday reality they represent into contact with an irrational world of fears, anxieties and pleasures.

Breton's analysis of the effects of this contact as "disorienting us in our memory by depriving us of a frame of reference" also has a strong resonance in Prendergast's work. Just as her maps and compasses lift us out of a recognizable terrain and strip away our reference points, so her objects undermine the quiet familiarity and reassurances we expect from domestic items. A well-worn table is metamorphosed by the addition of long tresses of hair – at once erotic and unsettling. The accompanying chair, with fine strands of hair sewn into its cushion, defies the simple act of sitting as it sprouts its own thatch of memories. No longer invisible items of furniture, the table and chair pitch us out of our comfort zones and make our world strange again. And, just as Prendergast's maps present emblems of free circulation, so her objects open channels of communication between the rational and the unconscious, providing access to areas of our emotional life that society generally considers taboo.

In this respect, many of the pieces possess an element of the theatrical prop or of a toy.

Love Table (detail)
1999

The *Prayer Gloves* and the *Grave Blanket* are waiting to be used or are mementos of a past performance, as is the brush and tress of *Love Object*. Similarly, Prendergast's furniture beckons the viewer, and the compass of *Lost* seems ready to be picked up before an unusual journey. This theatricality is simultaneously liberating and terrifying. It allows us to explore the potential of alternative lives and to remodel the world around us. At the same time it raises the suspicion that the everyday world is not as sure as it might seem and that our own personalities might be less fixed than we would like to believe.

In this way, the objects resemble the 'philosophical toys' of the nineteenth century – playthings (and parlour games) designed to instruct children in the laws governing the natural universe. Just as Prendergast's objects recall the wake games that wrestle with the fears and anxieties of death, so they also touch on the darker aspects of childhood. André Breton again, while discussing Picasso, noted the adult's continued fascination with toys:

> *When we were children we had toys that would make us weep with pity and anger today. One day, perhaps, we shall see the toys of our whole life spread before us like those of our childhood. It was Picasso who put this idea into my mind … We grow up until a certain age, it seems, and our playthings grow up with us, playing a part in the drama, whose only theatre is the mind.*

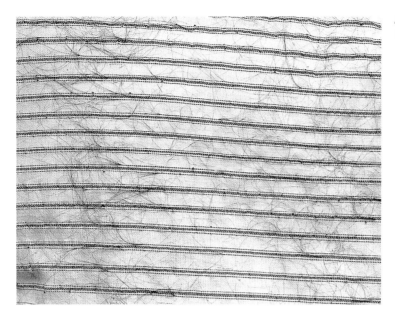

After (detail)
1999

That final image of the 'theatre of the mind' aptly describes the space conjured up by Prendergast's work. Pieces such as *Love Table*, *Prayer Gloves*, *After* and *Love Object* serve as the focus for stories and scenarios that bubble up from the unconscious, archetypal narratives stimulated to play themselves out in the viewer's mind. At times, the similarity to fairy tales is unmistakable. *Love Object*, for instance, with its rich, fine tress of hair and hairbrush, evokes traces of *Rapunzel* or *The Goose Girl* – stories with more than their share of darkness and death. Defending the sinister dimensions of the fairy tale, the psychoanalyst Bruno Bettelheim argues that

> *The dominant culture wishes to pretend, particularly where children are concerned, that the dark side of man does not exist, and professes a belief in an optimistic meliorism ... In practically every fairy tale good and evil are given body in the form of some figures and their actions, as good and evil are omnipresent in life and the propensities for both are present in every man ...*

In other words, the fairy tale introduces us as children to the dark side of human nature and to the inescapable fact of death. By couching its lessons in the irrational world of enchantment the genre allows its readers and listeners to confront and explore inner problems that do not conform to the dictates of reason.

Prendergast is able to tap into the power of such associations not only through the subject-matter of her work, but also, just as often, through her choice of material. *Love Table*, *Love Object*, *After* and *The End and The Beginning II* all use human hair – a powerful medium for Prendergast's concerns with memory, death, birth and renewal. Hair carries a strong symbolic load stretching back in time to the cult of the saintly relic and the more secular courtly tradition of presenting a lover with a locket of pubic hair. The metaphysical poet John Donne combined such references in his meditation on death entitled 'The Relic':

When my grave is broke up again
Some second guest to entertain,
(For graves have learned that woman-head
To be to more than one a bed)
And he that digs it, spies
A bracelet of bright hair about the bone,

Will he not let us alone,
And think that there a loving couple lies,
Who thought that this device might be some way
To make their souls, at the last busy day,
Meet at this grave, and make a little stay?

Even in less mythic realms, hair remains a material that embodies the concerns of Prendergast. In *A Natural History of the Senses*, Diane Ackerman points out that

Most people have about 100,000 hair follicles on their head, and lose between fifty and a hundred hairs a day through normal combing, brushing, or fussing. Each hair grows for only about two to six years, at about five or six inches a year, and then its follicle rests for a few months, the hair falls out, and is eventually replaced by a new hair. So when you see a beautiful head of hair, you're looking at hairs in many different stages in a complex system of growth, death, and renewal. Fifteen percent of it is resting at any one time, the other 85 percent growing; many dozens of hairs are all set to die tomorrow, and deep in the follicles new hairs are budding.

These natural processes of growth, death and renewal give Prendergast's work an unforced resonance. Moreover, the recent scientific unravelling of DNA strands and the mapping of genes in the Genome Project often find their focus in hair as it is one of the most accessible sources of human DNA. When Prendergast's spool of hair from her mother, herself and her son knowingly intertwines the family's generations, it also creates a genetic line of communication back through time, recording and preserving the artist's DNA. Like, the 'City Drawings', it opens channels of information, opposing entropy.

These works are so powerful because they can function at the level of myth, fairy tale or secular science. They seem at times to convey purely private codes and to spring from a solipsistic sense of making, yet they touch on public issues and operate on several levels of accessibility for everyone. It is possible to approach them as works grounded in archetypal imagery stretching back through time. Obversely, many of the works could be read through the prism of more recent histories. *The Endless Goodbye*, for example, has echoes of the noirish world of Philip Chandler, who spent his life writing of death under such titles as *The Long Goodbye* and *The Big Sleep*. *Secret Kiss*, too, could be seen as an inheritor of the Surrealist erotic object. On the other hand, it could be viewed within the context of Northern Ireland – the balaclava as terrorist mask, cheekily turned pink (who is kissing whom?). *Negative Space* and *Still Life* can fuel countless mythic readings or could be seen as inheritors of the art historical tradition of Nicolas Poussin's *The Arcadian Shepherds* – a monument to death centrally placed in a land of paradise. Poussin's shepherds attempt to understand that tomb's enigmatic motto '*et in arcadia ego*'; is the deceased happiest in the state of death?

Prendergast's works present us with the same enigmas. We are guided only by empty atlases and 'lost' has become such a desirable location that it is even marked on our compass dial.

Notes

Diane Ackerman, *A Natural History of the Senses*, London (Chapman) 1990

Sarane Alexandrian, *Surrealist Art*, London (Thames and Hudson) 1970

Nancy Andreasen, *The Broken Brain: The Biological Revolution in Psychiatry*, New York (Harper and Row) 1984, p. 125

Bruno Bettelheim, *The Uses of Enchantment: The Meaning and Importance of Fairy Tales*, Harmondsworth (Penguin) 1976

Santiago Ramón y Cajal, 'Drawing the Nerves', in *The Faber Book of Science*, ed. John Carey, London (Faber and Faber) 1995, p. 253

James Corner, 'The Agency of Mapping: Speculation, Critique and Invention', in *Mappings*, ed. Denis Cosgrove, London (Reaktion Books) 1999, pp. 213, 251

John Donne, *The Complete English Poems*, Harmondsworth (Penguin) 1971

Kynaston McShine (ed.), *Joseph Cornell*, New York (Museum of Modern Art) 1980

Armand Mattelart, 'Mappng, Modernity and Communication Networks', in *Mappings*, ed. Denis Cosgrove, London (Reaktion Books) 1999, p. 184

Peggy Phelan, *Mourning Sex: Performing Public Memories*, London (Routledge) 1997

Plates

Land (detail previous page)
1991
canvas, paint, tent poles
234 × 620 × 358 cm

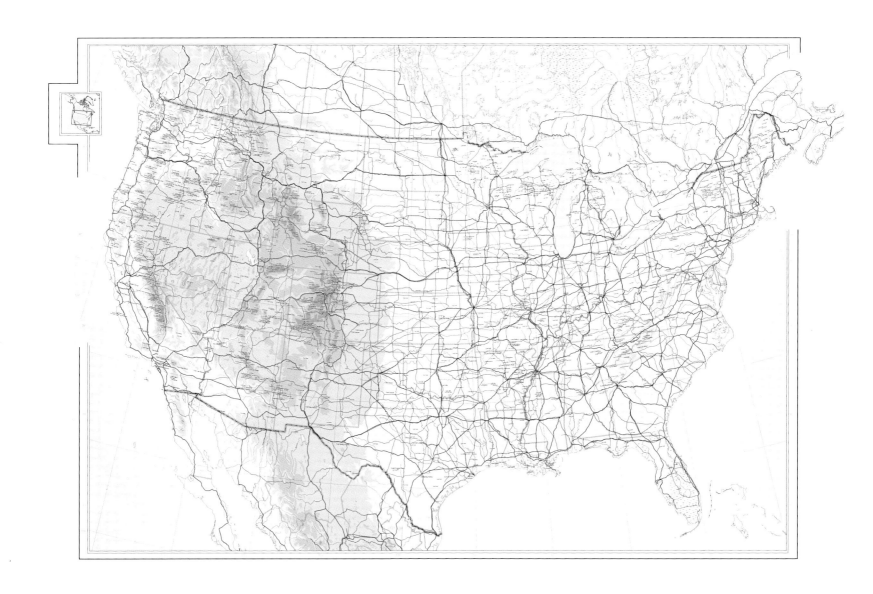

Lost
1999
computer-generated image on paper
85 × 132 cm

28

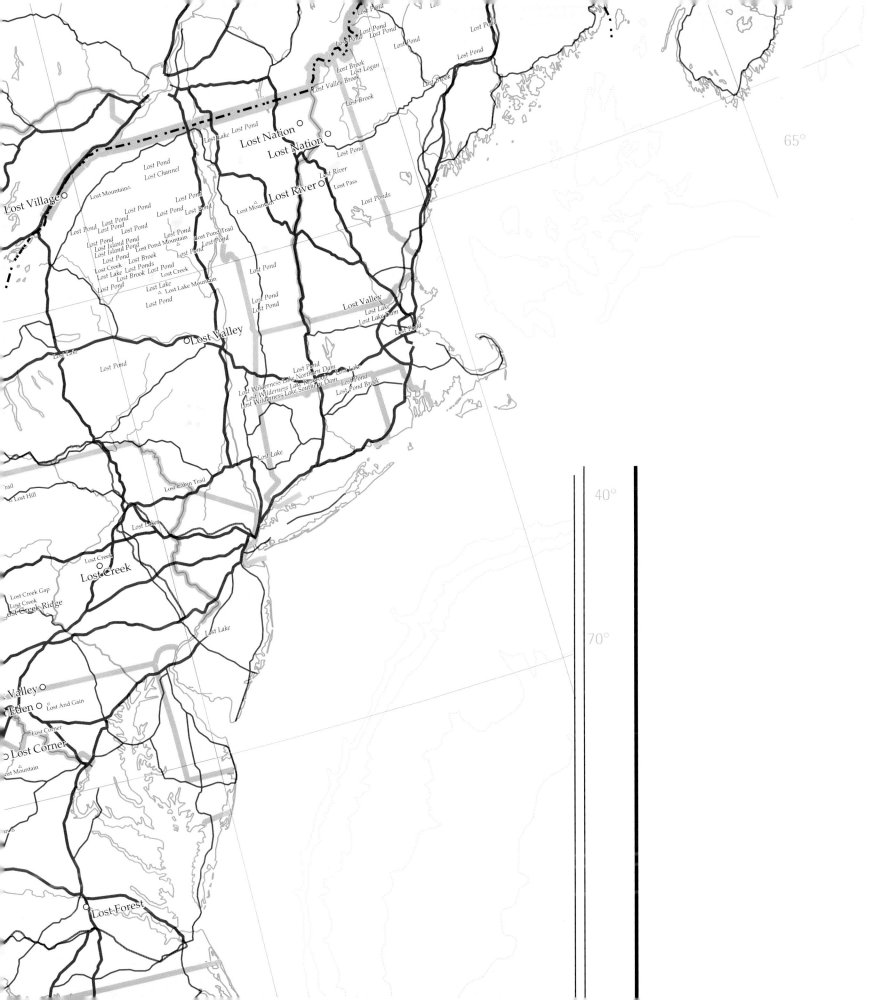

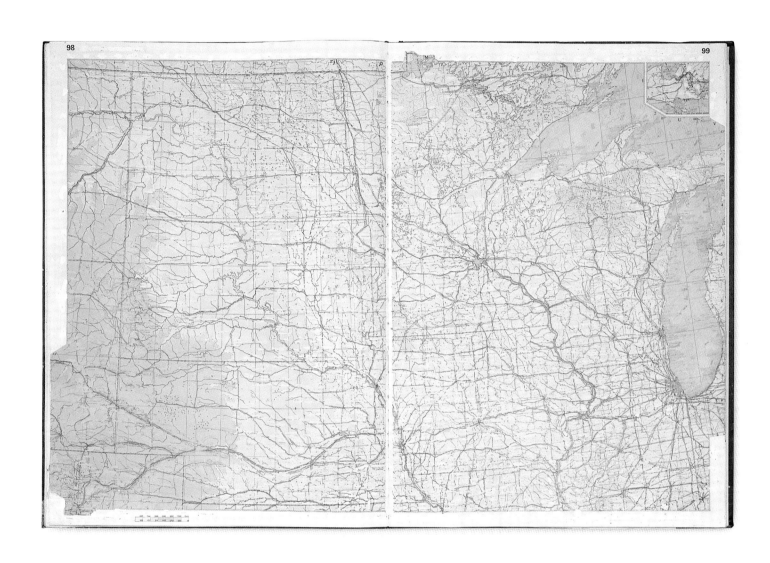

Empty Atlas (detail opposite page)
1999
The Times Atlas reworked by artist, acrylic paint
55 × 37.5 × 2 cm

'City Drawings'
1992 (ongoing series)
pencil on paper
24 × 32 cm

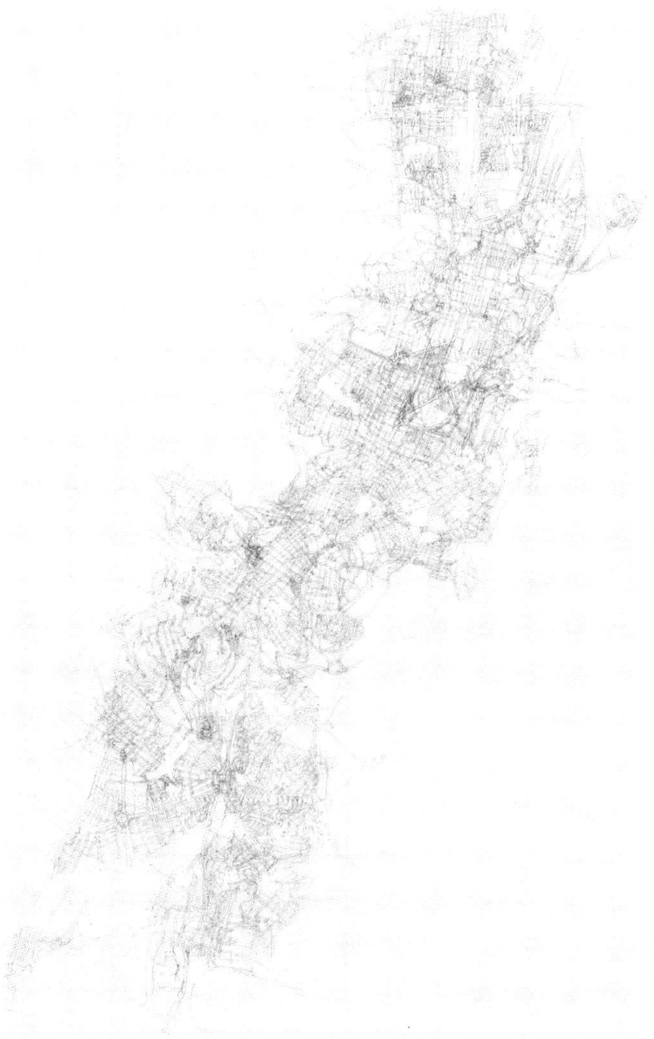

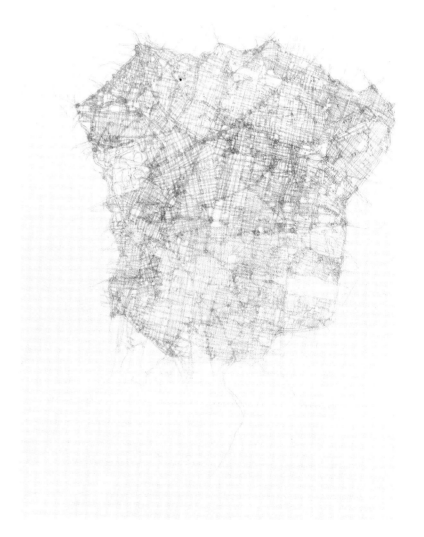

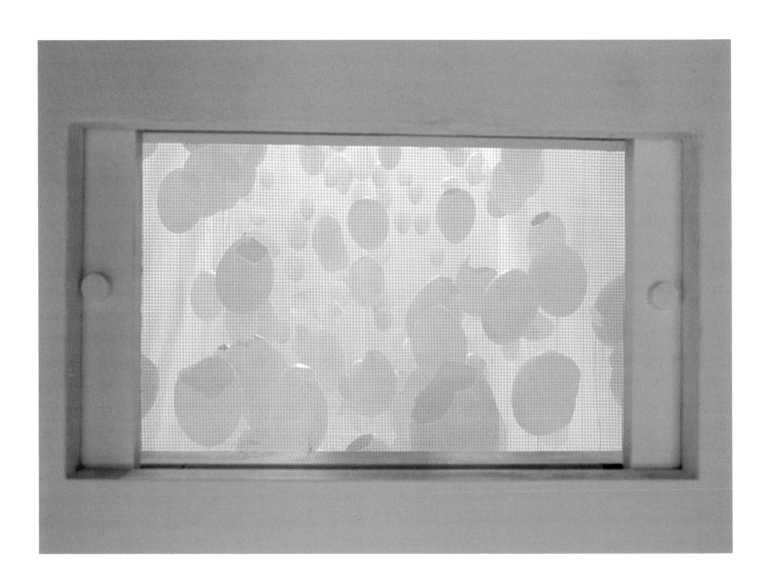

Still Life (detail opposite page)
1999
wood and eggs
74 × 206 × 198.5 cm

95

Untitled
1994
wool, filling and motor (baby's knitted jumper)
20 × 48 × 4 cm

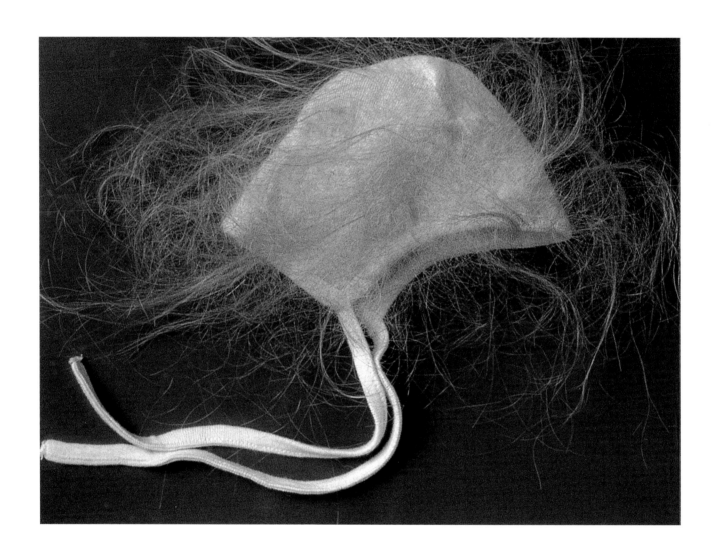

The End and The Beginning I
1997
cotton bonnet with human hair
display case 13 × 20 × 20 cm

98

The End and The Beginning II
1997
three generations of human hair
cotton reel and human hair
edition one of three
5.5 × 4 × 4 cm

99

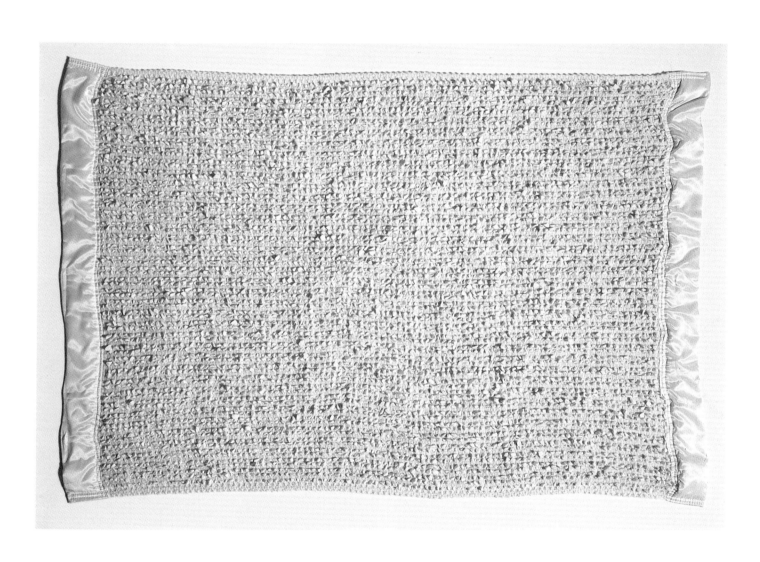

Grave Blanket (Version I) (detail opposite page)
1997
woollen blanket and marble chippings
108 × 71 cm

Love Table
1999
wood, fabric and human hair
table 26 × 63 × 71 cm; chair 36 × 54 × 91 cm

Love Object
1999
plastic brush, comb and human hair
67 × 28 × 5 cm

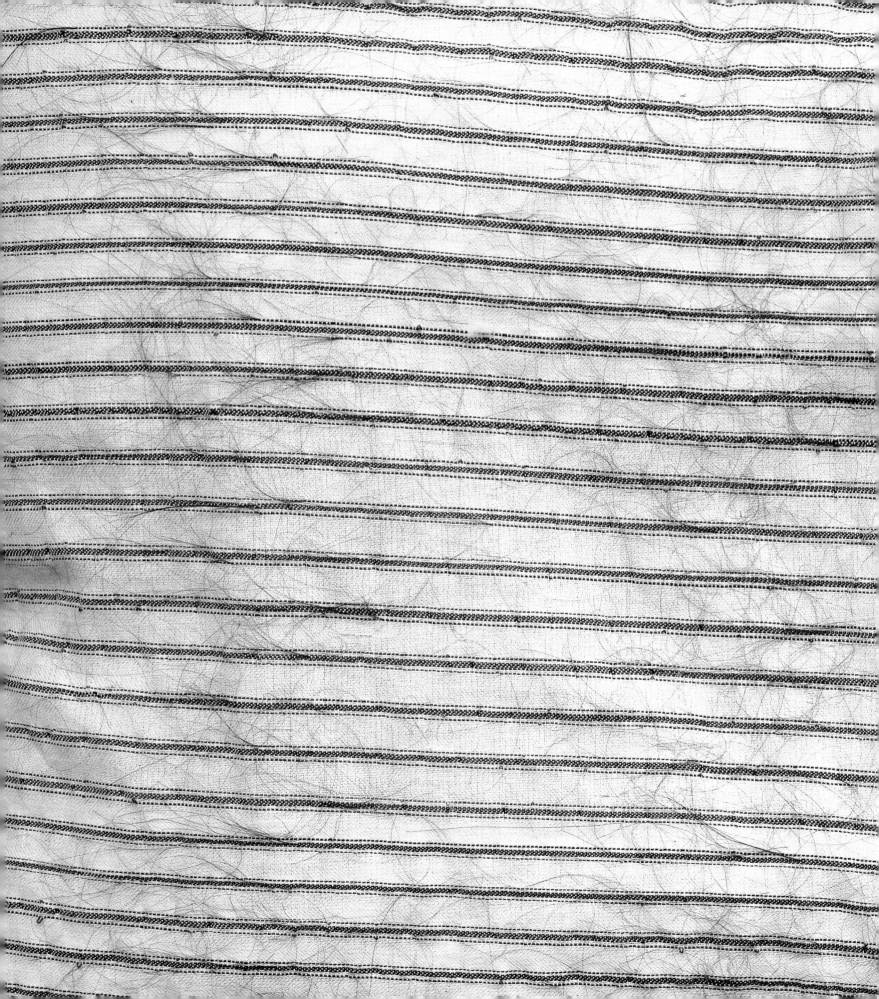

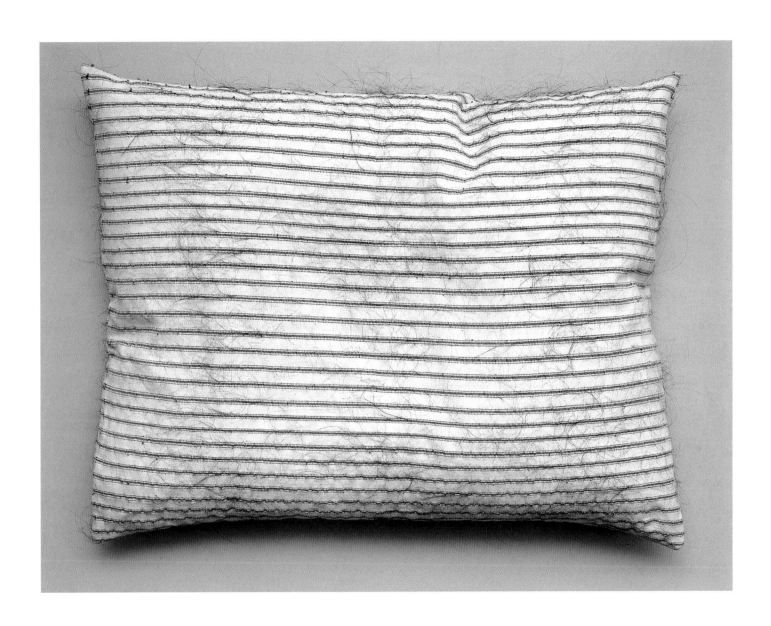

After (detail opposite page)
1999
woven cotton and human hair
42 × 55 × 11 cm

111

Secret Kiss (Version II)
1999
knitted wool
40×20×33cm

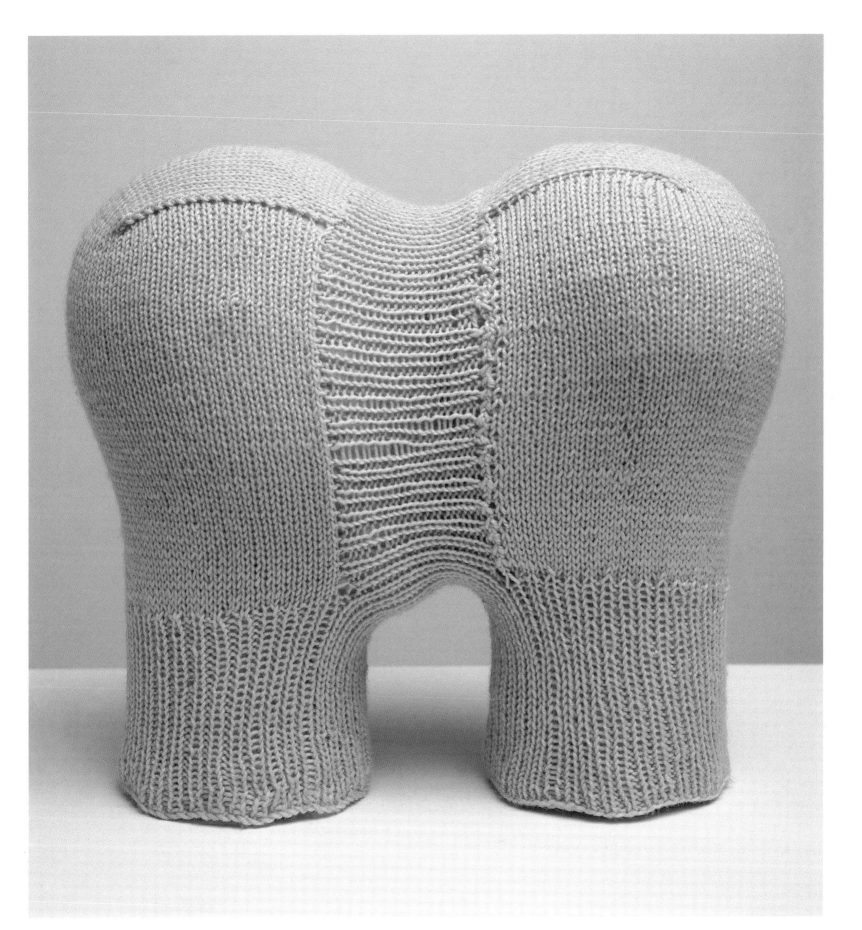

Checklist of works

Lost
1999
compass reworked by artist
6 × 4.5 × 1 cm
Courtesy of the artist and
Kerlin Gallery, Dublin
(Page 6)

Negative Space
1999
wood and wallpaper
installation dimensions
variable,
box 74 × 206 × 198.5 cm
Courtesy of the artist and
Kerlin Gallery, Dublin
(Page 15: detail)

Land *
1991
canvas, paint, tent poles
234 × 620 × 358 cm
Collection Arts Council
of Great Britain
(Pages 25, 26)

Lost *
1999
computer-generated image
on paper
85 × 132 cm
Courtesy of the artist and
Kerlin Gallery, Dublin
(Pages 28–33)

Empty Atlas *
1999
The Times Atlas reworked by
artist, acrylic paint
55 × 37.5 × 2 cm
Courtesy of the artist and
Kerlin Gallery, Dublin
(Pages 34, 35)

'City Drawings'
1992
(ongoing series)
pencil on paper
24 × 32 cm
Collection Irish Museum
of Modern Art, Dublin
(Pages 36–92)

Still Life
1999
wood and eggs
74 × 206 × 198.5 cm
Courtesy of the artist and
Kerlin Gallery, Dublin
(Pages 94, 95)

Untitled
1994
wool, filling and motor
(baby's knitted jumper)
20 × 48 × 4 cm
Anne and William J. Hokin
Collection
(Page 97)

**The End and
The Beginning I**
1997
cotton bonnet with
human hair
display case 13 × 20 × 20 cm
Courtesy of Trish Bransten
and Dennis Gallagher
(Page 98)

**The End and
The Beginning II**
1997
three generations of
human hair
cotton reel and human hair
edition one of three
5.5 × 4 × 4 cm
Collection of the Arts
Council/An Chomhairle
Ealaíon
(Page 99)

Grave Blanket (Version I)
1997
woollen blanket and marble
chippings
108 × 71 cm
Courtesy of Kerlin Gallery,
Dublin
(Page 101)

Prayer Gloves
1998
wool
28 × 12 × 14 cm
Courtesy of the artist and
Kerlin Gallery, Dublin
(Page 103)

The Endless Goodbye
1998
set of two photographs
edition of three
each 13 × 9.5 cm (unframed)
Private collection
(Pages 104, 105)

Love Table
1999
wood, fabric and human hair
table 26 × 63 × 71 cm
chair 36 × 54 × 91 cm
Courtesy of B Nadal-Ginard
and Laura Steinberg
(Page 107)

Love Object
1999
plastic brush, comb
and human hair
67 × 28 × 5 cm
Courtesy of the artist and
Kerlin Gallery, Dublin
(Page 109)

After
1999
woven cotton and human
hair
42 × 55 × 11 cm
Courtesy of the artist and
Kerlin Gallery, Dublin
(Pages 110, 111)

Secret Kiss (Version II)
1999
knitted wool
40 × 20 × 33 cm
Courtesy of the artist and
Kerlin Gallery, Dublin
(Page 113)

Lakes of Ireland **
1998
(seris of 4)
pencil on paper
24 × 32 cm
Collection of John Hannan

Rivers of Ireland **
1999
(series of 4)
pencil on paper
24 × 32 cm
Courtesy of the artist and
Kerlin Gallery, Dublin

Biography

1958   Born Dublin
1976–1980   National College of Art and Design, Dublin
1982–1983   National College of Art and Design, Dublin
1983–1986   Royal College of Art, London
            Currently lives and works in London

Solo Exhibitions

1999–2000   *The End and The Beginning*, Irish Museum of
            Modern Art, Dublin
1997   *City Drawings*, Art Now Project Room,
            Tate Gallery, London
            Angles Gallery, LA International, Los Angeles.
1994   Peter Scott Gallery, Lancaster
            Royal Festival Hall, South Bank Centre, London.
1991   Camden Arts Centre, London
1990   Douglas Hyde Gallery, Dublin, and tour.
1987   Unit 7 Gallery, London
            Henry Moore Foundation Fellow Exhibition,
            Camberwell School of Arts and Crafts, London

Selected Group Exhibitions

1999   *The Lie of the Land*, John Hansard Gallery,
            Southampton
            Irish Art Now: From the Poetic to the Political
            organized by Independent Curators
            International, USA, with the Irish Museum of
            Modern Art, Dublin, touring to McMullen
            Museum of Art, Boston College; Art Gallery of
            Newfoundland and Labrador, St John's; Chicago
            Cultural Center; and elsewhere in the USA
            0044: Irish Artists in Britain, PS1, New York and
            Allbright-Knox Art
            Gallery, Buffalo, and Crawford Municipal Art
            Gallery, Cork
            Multiplesx2, Temple Bar Galleries and Studios,
            Dublin, curated by Jeremy Millar
            Perceptual Engineering, London

1998   *Paved with Gold*, Kettle's Yard, Cambridge
            Robert Miller Gallery, New York
            Kerlin Gallery, Dublin
            Here to Stay, Arts Council Collection,
            Purchases of the 1990s. Exhibition toured by
            National Touring Exhibitions, England
            Memento Metropolis, Stockholm
1997   *Magnetic* (Kathy Prendergast, Callum Innes,
            Juliao Sarmento,Helmet Dorner and Ed
            Ruscha), Sean Kelly Gallery, New York
            Selections Fall '97, Drawing Center, New York
            Re/Dressing Kathleen, McMullen Museum of
            Art, Boston College
            Irish Geographies, Djanogly Art Gallery,
            Nottingham
            The Curiosity Room, Jack Shainman Gallery,
            New York
            At One Remove, Henry Moore Institute, Leeds
            Residue, Douglas Hyde Gallery, Dublin
            Kerlin Gallery, Dublin
            Laughter – Ten Years After, Beaver College Art
            Gallery, Spruance Art Centre, Glenside,
            Philadelphia
1996   *Memento Metropolis*, Copenhagen
1995–1996   *Poetic Land – Political Territory*, NCCA touring
            exhibition
            Irish Representative at Venice Biennale.
1994   *Well-Spring*, Bath Festival
            Summer Show, Kerlin Gallery, Dublin.
            From Beyond the Pale, Irish Museum of
            Modern Art, Dublin
1993   *Dorothy Cross, John Kindness and Kathy
            Prendergast*, Kerlin Gallery,Dublin
1992   *Journeys*, Winchester Art Gallery and tour.
1991   *Inheritance and Transformation*, Irish
            Museum of Modern Art, Dublin
            Edge to Edge: Three Sculptors from Ireland,
            Konstallen Sandviken and Kulturhuset, Sweden
            *Irish Art of The Eighties – Nature and
            Culture*, Douglas Hyde Gallery, Dublin
            The Upturned Ark, Pitt Rivers Museum, Oxford
            Strongholds, New Art from Ireland, Tate
            Gallery Liverpool and tour

1988	*Heads Exhibition*, The Arts Council, Dublin and tour
	ROSC 88, Guinness Hop Store, Dublin
	A Sense of Place, Battersea Arts Centre, London
1988	*Open Futures*, Ikon Gallery, Birmingham
1987	*Eighty*, Les Peintures d'Europe, Strasbourg
	Irish Women Artists, Douglas Hyde Gallery, Dublin
	Chisenhale Gallery, London
1987	Paris Biennale
	Joyce Centenary Exhibition, Douglas Hyde Gallery, Dublin
1986	*Bursary Show*, The Arts Council, Dublin
	Decade Show, NCAD, Guinness Hop Store, Dublin
	Celtic Vision, Centro del Cultural Conde Duque, Madrid, and tour
1985	*Drawings*, Hendriks Gallery, Dublin
1984	*Christmas Show*, Hendriks Gallery, Dublin
	4 Women, Hendriks Gallery, Dublin
1983	*Guinness Peat Aviation Awards Exhibition*, Douglas Hyde Gallery, Dublin
1982	10 on 8 Exhibition Space, New York

Awards

1995	Premio 2000, Venice Biennale
1992	Rome Award in Sculpture, British School in Rome
1990	Arts Council of Ireland Bursary
1988	Macauley Fellowship, Arts Council of Ireland.
1986	Royal College of Art Travel Award
	Henry Moore Foundation Fellowship, Camberwell School of Arts and Crafts, London
1986	Guinness Peat Aviation Award for Emerging Artists
1984	Arts Council of Ireland Bursary
1983	Guinness Peat Aviation Award for Emerging Artists
1982	Arts Council of Ireland Travel Grant
	Alice Berger Hammerschlager Travel Grant

Commissions

1997	'Inserts', The Laboratory, Ruskin School of Art, University of Oxford (an artists' publication in the geographical journal *Society in Space*)

Collections

AIB Bank
Arts Council of England
Arts Council of Ireland/An Chomhairle Ealaíon
American Express
Guinness (Irl) Ltd
Hugh Lane Municipal Gallery of Modern Art, Dublin
Irish Museum of Modern Art, Dublin
The Contemporary Museum Honolulu
Cheekwood Museum of Art, Nashville
Santa Barbara University Art Museum
Private collections in Ireland, Great Britain, Europe and USA

Bibliography

Catalogues

Irish Art Now: From the Poetic to the Political by Declan McGonagle, Fintan O'Toole and Kim Levin, Merrell Holberton and Independent Curators International, 1999
0044: Irish Artists in Britain, Crawford Municipal Art Gallery, Cork, and tour
At One Remove, Henry Moore Institute, Leeds, November 1997
Here to Stay, Arts Council Collection, Purchases of the 1990s
Memento Metropolis, Copenhagen 1997
Art Now by Frances Morris, Tate Gallery, London, 1997
Irish Geographies, Djanogly Art Gallery, Nottingham, 1997
Irish Arts Review, vol. 13, 1997
Modern Art in Ireland by Dorothy Walker, 1997
Langage, Cartographie et Pouvoir, Orchard Gallery, Derry, 1996
Shane Cullen / Kathy Prendergast, Venice Biennale, 1995
Poetic Land – Political Territory, Northern Centre for Contemporary Art, Sunderland, 1995
From Beyond the Pale, Irish Museum of Modern Art, Dublin, 1994
Well-Spring, Bath Festival, 1994
Spotlight, Arts Council of Great Britain Collection, 1993
Art Inc., Gandon Publications, 1992
Edge to Edge, Gandon Editions, 1991
Strongholds exhibition, Tate Gallery Liverpool, February 1991
Range, Camden Arts Centre, November 1991
Inheritance and Transformation, Irish Museum of Modern Art, Dublin, May 1991
A New Tradition, Douglas Hyde Gallery, Dublin, 1990–91
Irish Art: The European Dimension, RHA Gallery, June – July 1990
Kathy Prendergast by Conor Joyce, Douglas Hyde Gallery, Dublin, 1990
Modern Art Collection by David Scott, Trinity College, Dublin, 1990
Kathy Prendergast, Douglas Hyde Gallery, Dublin, 1990
ROSC 88 catalogue, Guinness Hop Store, Dublin, 1988
Irish Women Artists, National Gallery and Douglas Hyde Gallery, Dublin
Portfolio, ed. John O'Regan
Irish Sculpture from 1600 to the Present Day by Anne Crookshank, 1984
GPA Tulfarris Show catalogue, 1983
Contemporary Irish Art by Roderic Knowles, Dublin (Wolfhound Press) 1982

Reviews

Out of the Void, *Contemporary Visual Arts*, 17, 1998
Kathy Prendergast and Dorothy Cross, Angles Gallery, LA, 1997
Soo Jin Kim, *Art Issues*, September 1997
Susan Kandell, *LA Times*, 25 July 1997
Sarah Kent, Tate Gallery, *Time Out* [London], 30 April – 7 May 1997
Medb Ruane, Tate Gallery, *The Sunday Times* [London], 1997
Helen Swords, Tate Gallery, *Circa*, no. 80, 1997
Tate Gallery, *Contemporary Visual Arts* [London], 15, 1997, p.71
Tate Gallery, *The Big Issue* [London], 10 March 1997
Ian Fox, Orfeo Opera Theatre Company, *Sunday Tribune*, November 1995
Fintan O'Toole, Orfeo Opera Theatre Company, *Irish Times*, November 1995

Michael Dervan, Orfeo Opera Theatre Company, *Irish Times*, November 1995

Mic Moroney, Venice Biennale, *Sunday Times*, 1995

Michael Kimmelman, Venice Biennale, *New York Times*, 9 July 1995

Ciara Ferguson, Venice Biennale, *Irish Independent*, June 1995

Medb Ruane, Venice Biennale, *Sunday Times*, June 1995

Luke Clancy, Venice Biennale, *Irish Times*, 22 June 1995

William Packer, Venice Biennale, *Financial Times*, 20 June 1995

William Feaver, Venice Biennale, *The Observer* [*Review* section], 18 June 1995

John McEwen, Venice Biennale, *Sunday Telegraph*, 18 June 1995

Aidan Dunne, Venice Biennale, *Sunday Tribune*, 18 June 1995

Venice Biennale, *The Economist*, 17 June 1995

Paddy Agnew, Venice Biennale, *Irish Times*, 13 June 1995

Luke Clancy, Venice Biennale, *Irish Times*, 13 June 1995

Venice Biennale, *The Observer*, 11 June 1995

Brian Fallon, Sligo Connections, Model Arts Centre, Sligo, *Irish Times*, July 1995

Aidan Dunne, Sligo Connections, Model Arts Centre, Sligo, *Sunday Tribune*, July 1995

Siraz Izhar, Edge in the Centre: Irish Artists in London, *Circa*, no. 60, 1993

Aidan Dunne, John Kindness, Dorothy Cross, Kathy Prendergast, Kerlin Gallery, Dublin, *Sunday Tribune*, 1993

Tom Lubbock, Strongholds exhibition, Tate Gallery Liverpool, *Independent on Sunday*, February 1991

Brian Fallon, Strongholds exhibition, Tate Gallery Liverpool, *Irish Times*, 27 February 1991

Aidan Dunne, Exhibition, Douglas Hyde Gallery, Dublin, *Sunday Tribune*, 1990

John Hutchinson, Exhibition, Douglas Hyde Gallery, Dublin, *Irish Times*, 1990

Exhibition, Douglas Hyde Gallery, Dublin, *In Dublin*, 1990

Aidan Dunne, Arts Council Heads, *Sunday Tribune*, 1988

Brian Fallon, Arts Council Heads, *Irish Times*, 1988

Brian Fallon, ROSC 88, *Irish Times*, 1988

Déaglán de Bréadún, ROSC 88, *Irish Times*, 1988

Aidan Dunne, ROSC 88, *Sunday Tribune*, 21 August 1988

Aidan Dunne, Irish Women Artists, Douglas Hyde Gallery, *Sunday Press*, 1987

Hilary Pyle, Arts Council Bursary Show, *Irish Times*, 1987

Dorothy Walker, European Painting of the Eighties, 1987

Brian Fallon, Arts Council Bursary Show, *Irish Times*, 1986

Brian Fallon, Kathy Prendergast and Richard Gorman exhibition, Hendriks Gallery, Dublin, *Irish Times*, 16 July 1985

Aidan Dunne, Four Women Exhibition, Hendriks Gallery, Dublin, *Sunday Press*, 4 August 1984

Ciaran MacGonigal, Four Women Exhibition, Hendriks Gallery, Dublin, *Field & Countryside Magazine*, August 1984

Brian Fallon, Four Women Exhibition, Hendriks Gallery, Dublin, *Irish Times*, July 1984

John Meany, Four Women Exhibition, Hendriks Gallery, Dublin, *In Dublin*, July 1984

John Hutchinson, NCAD Final Degree Show, *Irish Times*, 1983

Brian Fallon, GPA Tulfarris Show, *Irish Times*, 1983

Desmond McAvock, Joyce Centenary

Exhibition, Douglas Hyde Gallery, Dublin, *Irish Times*, 1982

Anne Harris, Joyce Centenary Exhibition, Douglas Hyde Gallery, Dublin, *Image Magazine*, 1982

Hilary Pyle, Paris Biennale, 1982, *Cork Examiner*, 25 November 1982

Marina Vaisey, Paris Biennale, 1982, *The Sunday Times*, 31 October 1982

Tulfarris Environmental Sculpture, *Sunday Press*, 7 June 1981

Tulfarris Environmental Sculpture, *Sunday Independent*, 31 May 1981

Tulfarris Environmental Sculpture, *Irish Times*, 23 May 1981 (photo: Tom Lawlor)

Ciaran Carty, Tulfarris Environmental Sculpture, *Sunday Independent*, May 1981

Independent Artists, *In Dublin*, 14–27 November 1980

Aidan Dunne, Independent Artists, *Sunday Tribune*, 9 November 1980

Independent Artists, *Sunday Independent*, November 1980

Living Arts Awards, *Irish Independent, Art View*, 7 September 1980

Kate Robinson, Living Arts Awards, Hibernia, 1 September 1980

Annette Blackwell, Living Arts Awards, *Irish Independent*, August 1980

Ronan Farren, Living Arts Awards, *Evening Herald*, 14 August 1980

Seamus Martin, Living Arts Awards: *Evening Herald*, 14 August 1980

Living Arts Awards, *Irish Press*, 14 August 1980